How To Buy Bitcoin:
A Beginner's Guide to Cryptocurrency Investing

Copyright © 2018 Monte Werle. All rights reserved.

No portion of this book may be reproduced, stored in a retrieval system, or transmitted in any form or by any means--electronic, mechanical, photocopy, recording, scanning, or other--except for brief quotations in critical reviews or articles, without the prior written permission of the publisher.

The scanning, uploading, or distribution of this book via the internet or any other means without the express permission of the publisher is illegal and punishable by law. Please purchase only authorized electronic editions of this work and do not participate in or encourage piracy of copyrighted materials, electronically or otherwise. Your support of the author's rights is appreciated.

This publication is designed to provide accurate and authoritative information in regard to the subject matter covered. It is sold with the understanding that the publisher is not engaged in rendering legal, accounting, or other professional service. If legal advice or other expert assistance is required, the services of a competent professional person should be sought.

LIMIT OF LIABILITY / DISCLAIMER

The information in this book is intended to improve beginning investors' understanding of putting money into cryptocurrencies. Nothing in this book constitutes investment, legal, or tax advice. The information in this book should not be construed as any endorsement, recommendation or sponsorship of any company, strategy, investment, cryptocurrency coin, or exchange. There are risks in relying on information found on this book, and you must be sure you understand these risks before using any information in this book. You should evaluate the information made available in this book, and you should seek the advice of professionals to evaluate any information, opinions, services, products or other information found herein. While the author/publisher have used the best efforts in preparing this book, they make no representations or warranties with respect to the accuracy or completeness of this book and specifically disclaim any implied warranties merchability or fitness for a particular purpose. No warranty may be created or extended by sales representatives or written sales materials. The strategies contained herein may not be suitable for your situation. You should consult with a professional where appropriate. Neither the publisher nor the author shall be liable for any loss of profit or any other commercial damages, including but not limited to special, incidental, consequential, or other damages.

DEDICATION

This book is dedicated to my amazing family. I love you all so much. Gladys, you are the love of my life. Your support in all of my ventures means the world to me. To Jasmine, Collin, Landon, and Brody, my beautiful children and future entrepreneurs.

Table of Contents

Taking the Mystery out of Cryptocurrency 9
Types of Cryptocurrencies 10
Block Chain Technology Crash Course 11
What Block Chain Means for Cryptocurrency Investors 11
How to Buy Cryptocurrencies on an Exchange 13
Fees for Trading 14
Using Trends to Your Advantage 15
Being an Investor vs. Being a Miner 17
The Benefits of Cryptocurrencies 17
The Risks 19
The Impact of Cryptocurrencies 22
Problems Cryptocurrencies Need to Solve 23
Investing Strategies 24
A Word About Charts 29
Tax Considerations 29
The Future 30
Conclusion 34
REFERENCE PAGE 38

How To Buy Bitcoin:

A Beginner's Guide to Cryptocurrency Investing

Copyright 2018 © Monte Werle

Taking the Mystery out of Cryptocurrency

Cryptocurrency, such as Bitcoin and Litecoin, mystifies many potential investors. To some cynical types, cryptocurrency sounds like fake money people use online. Many ask themselves why they would ever invest in the digital equivalent of something they consider to be no more valuable than Monopoly money.

Like so many new technologies, the mystery surrounding cryptocurrency disappears once you examine it more closely. Let's start by understanding the "crypto" part. This prefix basically refers to encryption, which is the process of scrambling information before it is transmitted so that nosy people and crooks can't read it. Only the receiver has the key to decrypt it. But don't worry about encryption, as you won't actually be doing this.

Here is a surprise for you: You have more than likely been using something like cryptocurrencies all your life. You probably receive your paycheck electronically, then use a debit card to spend that money electronically. Your purchase amounts are sent through encrypted channels from the merchant to your bank, which then processes the purchase amount and credits the merchant for the transaction, minus any fees. No paper or actual currency ever exchanges hands. It is simply an exchange of an agreed-upon value.

So you see, the idea of electronic currency is not strange or new at all.
When you buy cryptocurrencies, you are purchasing a digital representation of a monetary value. It has no physical form like the change or bills in your wallet, so it may seem strange to people who like to have a little jingle in their pocket. When you buy cryptocurrency, the amount you paid for it becomes its monetary value, at least until market conditions start to move that value either up or down.

Let's use the example of Ethereum. Say you bought in for $715. That's the price for one "coin." Like stocks on any of the stock exchanges, the value of an Ethereum coin (or any cryptocurrency) fluctuates daily. When more buyers come into the market seeking to purchase a coin than there are coins to sell, the price per coin rises. People who owns coins know these market conditions may indicate a good time to sell some of their holdings in order to cash in on the higher price generated by increased demand, thus increasing their return on their initial investment. In a sellers' market, sellers have more customers to choose from and market prices rise accordingly.

Conversely, if too many people are trying to sell coins at the same time, many potential buyers feel like they can wait for the price of the coins to further drop before investing in the market.

While you do need to be aware of how the market moves and the factors that may affect it, you don't worry about all that. Just realize that the value of your coin may change. If it drops, you may want to sell it and keep as much of your money as you can. Or you might want to hang on to it and see if the price bounces back up. If the price goes up, you can sell it then and take your profits.

That is trading cryptocurrencies in a nutshell.

As Warren Buffett famously said, "Don't invest in something you don't understand." In this book, you will learn the ins and outs of trading these currencies, along with some wise tips for beginners. You will gain a knowledge of how the cryptocurrencies world works. You'll be ahead of those that just jump in and lose their shirts on the first trade.

Here is what you will learn on your way to mastering the art of investing in Cryptocurrencies:

The Types of Cryptocurrencies
What Blockchain Technology Means for Investors
How to Use an Exchange for Purchases
Using Trends to Your Advantage
Being an Investor vs. Being a Miner
The Risks Involved
Tax Considerations
Fees for Trading
Preparing for the Future of Cryptocurrency Investing

Types of Cryptocurrencies

The digital environment for cryptocurrencies is changing so fast that a list of such currencies would be out of date by the time you read this book. What is important to know is that many types of currencies exist.

For example, some are designed to help corporations settle contracts, while others are used by banks to make payments. There is a dental currency, and one to process exchanges between machines. Another one is geared toward buying and selling legal marijuana.

Freicoin was designed to lose value. It's probably not a good idea to invest in that one. Solarcoin is for energy producers who offer renewable energy. And of course, it had to happen: XRP was created to connect all the other currencies so people can make trades and exchanges between currencies.

The point is not how many types of cryptocurrency there are. Just realize that some will come and go quickly, and some are not suitable for trading. It's hard to imagine the dental currency lasting, and investing in a currency for processing machine transactions would require knowing there is an increasing demand.

As a beginner, your best strategy is to invest in something that has caught the interest of other investors. In other words, other people should have invested at least a billion dollars' worth of their money before you, as a beginning investor, put a dime of your money into it.

Of course, the opposite strategy could work. You could find a newcomer to the market with a low initial value and buy it hoping that it will skyrocket. Sometimes this strategy pays off handsomely. Sometimes you just lose your money.

A Beginner's Guide to Cryptocurrency Investing

The types of cryptocurrencies can be divided into those with the highest value, mid-value ones, and low-value ones. This may be a more useful way to look at them than what clientele they appeal to.

There are cryptocurrencies designed to have special technological features. Some use new algorithms, new types of security, and innovative ways to calculate value. You shouldn't worry about any of that as a beginner. Don't let it scare you off. You know techies, they love to talk about all their new gadgets and networks, and bells and whistles.

There is one type of cryptocurrency that does not exist: a low-risk one. Prices bounce around out there and you could get bucked off like a cowboy at a rodeo. We will be talking about risk and risk tolerance later, but for now, just know that this is a high-risk investment. You should also know that the higher the risk, the greater the potential profit.

Block Chain Technology Crash Course

Next, we are going to talk about block chain. This a virtually unbreakable encryption technology that is was invented by the individual or group that created Bitcoin to protect digital currency transfers. Block chain is basically a digital spreadsheet that permanently records transactions. It uses a dedicated system of linked computers called nodes, each containing identical copies of the virtual block chain ledger, to verify business transactions whether they involve the transfer of currency, the signing of contracts, or other important business functions. Each ledger on every connected computer updates continuously so that all the ledgers remain reconciled at all times. Once a transaction is completed, it is added to the block chain and cannot be changed or deleted.

Block chain technology is revolutionizing the business world, so you owe it to yourself to understand it. Of course, it is essential to investing in cryptocurrencies as well. Don't let the concept scare you off. You've survived 3D printing and appliances that can send you messages. You can handle block chain.

Soon you'll be tossing out phrases like "Bitcoin mining" and "Litecoin" at parties and everyone will think you're a genius.

What Block Chain Means for Cryptocurrency Investors

You may have heard a lot of people using the phrase "block chain" and thought you were becoming an old fogey who wasn't keeping up with technology. The tech world changes so fast. Not only are people using this word, it seems to have something to do with Bitcoin.

Let's take the confusion out of block chain. If you are wondering where the word comes from, it comes out of some techie's head, someone who wanted a cool-sounding word. Don't worry about blocks and chains. Here is what it really is: it's a record of transactions that no one central organization controls.

Here's how things used to work. Say you were trading stocks using an online broker. You would be able to see your transactions on your account, and no one else's. Only the broker would be able to tell who was trading.

How To Buy Bitcoin

With block chain, you can see everyone's transactions in your peer-to-peer network. No broker controls who sees what. And no broker certifies transactions. In other words, when you buy, you deal directly with the person selling, and vice versa. All trades are transparent to everyone at the same time, and the records of those transactions never disappear. By the way, even though the transactions are visible, you never know the identity of the people making those transactions.

Think of it like the first days of the Internet. Before the Internet, people received magazines and newspapers written by professional journalists in the mail, delivered to their doorsteps by a paper boy, or bought them from newsstands. Information came to you from publications where editors controlled what writers wrote about through the use of assignments, and writers gathered all the information for you. You didn't write any information yourself, because that job was for the professionals.

Suddenly the internet made everyone a writer. You could write an article and send it around the world to anyone who wanted it, with no publisher, and no editor to stop you or say you didn't have permission.

Think about money transactions in a similar way. Until now, if you wanted to buy something or send someone money, you had to write a check or use a debit card from your bank. Your bank would send the other person's bank the money, and the receiving person would retrieve it from his bank account.

Now, take out those banks, and imagine you can just send money directly to someone. No middleman, no delays. Presto! The other person gets the money in seconds and no bank had to handle it.

So it is with block chain. When you want to buy, your request goes out to a peer-to-peer network and a seller who likes the offer you have made sells you your requested Bitcoin. Your completed transaction or "block" is put together with a lot of other completed transactions into a "block chain" of data where it is permanently stored.

Ok, I know I said not to worry about chains and blocks, but that was just to keep you from throwing your hands up and saying, "I quit." But now that you know that your transaction is stored in blocks of data that are kept with other data blocks in a sequential chain, it's not so intimidating, is it?

Even with all of those mysterious words, it is still the same thing: direct, peer-to-peer buying and selling. No middle man.

So what?

Here is the best part. Once your completed transaction is in a block chain, everyone else on the network has an exact copy of that block chain.

Now say someone tries to take over your transaction that is in the block chain. All of the duplicates will show that one chain has been altered, and it will be rejected. The thief can't get away with hijacking your trades, because you have digital witnesses from all around the world.

A Beginner's Guide to Cryptocurrency Investing

The way it actually works is the block that breaks the rules of the chain gets labeled as invalid. This happens automatically.

Now that you know all of that, I hate to tell you, but you won't be using the information. All that blocking and chaining is done for you automatically when you trade cryptocurrencies. You can relax knowing that information about your trades is as well-protected as the gold in Fort Knox.

Also, if you memorize this section of the book, you can impress people at parties who ask, "What the heck is this block chain I keep hearing about?"

How to Buy Cryptocurrencies on an Exchange

Back in the day, people went to coin shops to buy collectible coins. You could hold them (they were covered in plastic) and examine them closely. Since cryptocurrencies only exist digitally, your "coin shop" will be an online exchange.

It is pretty simple to get started with an exchange. For example, you can use Coinbase to buy Bitcoin, Ethereum, Litecoin, or Bitcoin Cash (Many exchanges specialize in a few types of cryptocurrencies.)

Coinbase Is FDIC insured and the easiest way to turn fiat money (currency that the government has declared to be legal tender.) into cryptocurrency at the moment.

Now, if you remember what you learned about block chain, you know that the purchase of a crypto coin can't be reversed. This means the exchanges have to be very careful that they are not getting ripped off by bogus buyers.

And this means you are going to have to prove you are legit. But it's not really all that complicated. A credit card will help, along with a driver's license and some personal information the exchange will ask you for.

Just a quick aside about that credit card. You have to decide if you are a gambler or an investor. Getting all excited and maxing out your credit cards in hopes your cryptocurrency will soar is just not level-headed. Okay, sorry if I sounded like your mother. I just wanted to remind you that this is high-risk investing.

Back to the exchanges. Once you are cleared by the exchange, you can purchase your cryptocurrency.

Here are some other exchanges to think about.

Binance – My personal favorite exchange to buy alt coins
Kraken – Handles the same coins as Coinbase
Gemini – Similar to Kraken
Bittrex – Sells NEO
Polonex – May have newer coins
Livecoin – Another exchange that will have some variety

How To Buy Bitcoin

I will save your eyes from becoming bleary by not listing every exchange that is available. There are hundreds. The ones listed take U.S. dollars, but many exchanges have sprung up to take local currencies. From Australia to Korea, you can find exchanges that will accommodate any currency preference.

By the way, if you own coins you bought on Coinbase, you can transfer them to another exchange and buy a different type of coin.

So, you're ready to go. All you have to do is find an exchange, figure out how much a coin costs, and spend that much to own it. Right? Wrong.

Fees for Trading

You have to pay a commission to the exchange. You didn't think they were a charity, did you?

You will pay transaction fees. Ok, fine, you pay anywhere from 10 cents to four dollars in fees to buy a coin. The amount of the fee depends on which coin you buy. Now you decide to sell your coin. Guess what? You will pay a transaction fee to sell it.

Now follow this one. You buy coin A (transaction fee). You convert it to coin B (transaction fee for getting rid of coin A and a fee for buying coin B).

Just realize that a lot of buying and selling will rack up fees and eat into your profits or increase your losses.

Oh, by the way, transaction fees vary not only according to what kind of coin, but also the exchange you use. Shop around and compare fees.

So, we're almost through your first transaction. You know about exchanges and fees. Now for where to store your coins.

You need a wallet. You will find many online services offering to sell you a "wallet" where your coins can be put so no one can get at them.

I know it sounds strange, but it isn't. You already put information in the cloud. You can store your resume, your passwords, your will, or even Great Aunt Susie's recipe for brownies in the cloud. And you have security measures to keep people from getting into your files. This can include encryption, passwords, and anti-malware programs.

Storing coins is no different. You need an online address that is yours alone where you can store your coins. This needs to be secure, but you also need to be able to open it when you want to sell your coins or when you want to store coins you have purchased.

But here's the problem. A lot of scam artists offer fake online wallets. As soon as you store your coins, they take them and sell them.

So what do you do? First, you only deal with companies that have a stellar reputation.

A Beginner's Guide to Cryptocurrency Investing

A more reliable method is to use an app to store your coins. Apple and Android apps are everywhere, and you can download one to hold your coins. They come with security, and though they are still connected to the internet, they aren't as risky as storing your coins in someone else's online wallet service.

But here's another problem. The crooks have started selling fake apps. Your best bet it to find one with a solid reputation and stick with it.

There's an even better strategy. Store your coins on a USB device or external hard drive. This allows you to disconnect the device from the internet, so no hackers can get in. Of course, you can't trade with it locked away in your device either. So put just enough in an app so that you can trade, and keep the rest in your "hardware wallet," that is, your USB or hard drive. You can always transfer more coins to your app when you need to. But whatever you do, don't lose your USB, because if you do, the coins stored on it are gone forever. In fact, if you are the type who frequently loses your keys or your eyeglasses, I recommend that you don't use this technique without backing it up.

So you're all set. You know how to use an exchange to make purchases, watch out for big fees, and keep your coins safe in a wallet, app, or a USB drive. You've got the basics down.

Now let's learn how to jump into the pool without drowning. You need some trading strategies.

Using Trends to Your Advantage

The worst thing you can do is buy a cryptocurrency just before it dives in price. The best thing you can do is buy when it is at a low price and watch it rise to a new high.

Well, duh, you say. No kidding. But how do I do that?

With some solid concepts, you will intuitively know when to buy and sell. You just need some guidelines. Forget all the wise guys who have fancy trading tricks that "can't fail." You are about to get some no-nonsense ideas.

First, you need to find a chart that tracks the coin you are trading. These are all over the Internet. They are usually free. You just need a basic one, but try to find one that shows not only the price, but something called the on-balance volume indicator (OBV). Don't worry about what that is right now. Just get your chart with an OBV indicator and let's start learning.

There are two emotions that drive trading trends: fear and greed. People become afraid that the market will crash, so they sell. People get greedy and start chasing a coin that is increasing rapidly in price. They want in on the action before they miss out.

You, however, will be wiser than that. Why? Because you read this book. You can make a lot of money by staying off the emotional roller coaster.

Here's how:

How To Buy Bitcoin

A coin's price goes up when there are more buyers than sellers. Because sellers have so many customers to choose from, they keep raising their prices. Up goes the price, with buyers piling on to grab some of the wealth.

The uptrend will reverse when there are no more buyers. At some point, all those greedy customers will have bought up all the coins the sellers have. When everyone is a buyer, those buyers can't sell their coins to take their profits. There is no one left to sell to.

So what would you do? You would lower your price to attract a buyer. All the coin holders start lowering their prices so they can sell their coins and take their profits. At first, there are not many people who want to buy, so they keep lowering the price. More buyers come in, and the competition gets stiff, so people start lowering their prices dramatically. This is a crash in the making.

At some point, all the people who were trying to sell get rid of their coins, and the action slows down. A lot of people bought coins on the way down, and they are hoping the price comes back up so they can see their coins gain in value. Things stay quiet for a while but eventually new buyers come in, and the prices start going back up because there is more demand for the coins. Here we go again.

When you look at a price chart, don't look at numbers and lines, imagine what people are doing and why. This will help you understand the price action.

Get in at the beginning of an uptrend, but when you hear everybody saying, "You've got to buy this coin! It's going up like crazy!" that's when you realize that you are near the point where everyone is a buyer and no one is a seller. You are close to a top in the price. You can sell when everyone is saying, "buy" and avoid the downtrend that will come when there are no sellers left and there is no one to sell to. People will start lowering their prices.

When you hear everybody saying, "Sell, sell!" you know that everyone is going to become a seller soon and there will be no buyers for them to sell to. That's when you step in and become a buyer. You won't have much competition, and you'll get bargain prices.

Let everyone else get emotional. You just pounce when their emotions are at a peak.
But how do you know when emotions have reached a peak? That's where this on-balance volume indicator comes in.

Volume means how many coins are being bought and sold. A lot of volume means a lot of coins are being bought and low volume means fewer are getting bought.

So when volume is rising, the indicator's line starts rising. When volume is dropping, the indicator's line drops.

Now here's the fun part. When you see the price rising and the OBV dropping, that means fewer people are buying. The trend is running out of steam. Time to get out.

On the other hand, if you see the price drop and the OBV is going up, that means there are a lot of coins changing hands. Selling is accelerating. Wait for the price to start going back up on decent volume before you start buying.

Being an Investor vs. Being a Miner

I am only going to tell you about mining so you don't come across the word and say, "Hey, how come that book I read on cryptocurrency didn't mention this?"

A miner is someone who creates the blocks that go into the block chain.

Here is the basic process:

1. The miner gathers a set of transactions.
2. The miner makes sure the transactions are valid.
3. Now the transactions get put together in a block.
4. The last block in the chain gets fitted to the new block the miner created.
5. The miner solves a difficult mathematical problem called a proof of work.
6. The new block is added to the chain.

And there's one other thing you should know. The amount a miner gets paid goes down over time. When a coin is first issued, a miner gets a certain amount of money for each transaction (paid with the same coin the miner is working on). A limited amount of coins are issued. So each transaction reduces the number of coins available to pay miners from the original issue. As time passes, miners get paid less and less until eventually, all the coins are mined.

Now wait. I know you are getting ready to throw up your hands and say, " This is WAY over my head." Calm down. There's good news. You won't be doing any of this.

Why? Because it is not a good place for beginners to start. It is time-consuming, highly competitive, and even expensive. Yes, there are expenses involved.

So just realize miners make the blocks and don't worry about it.

Sheesh, you had me worried for a moment there. I thought you were going to stop reading.

The Benefits of Cryptocurrencies

Whenever you invest in anything, you should understand the demand for it. Look at why people want it and how it benefits them.

If you've heard of an investment "bubble" that breaks, realize that bubbles are formed when investors ignore the real demand for what they are investing in. In the case of cryptocurrencies, you have to determine whether they are a fad or whether they offer real value.

How To Buy Bitcoin

To be honest, no one really knows how to value cryptocurrencies right now. The best we can do is evaluate how they make people's lives easier or better. As time goes on, digital currencies will also have to provide superior characteristics like ease of transactions, speed of transactions, and automated record-keeping on a consistent basis.

Let's look at some of the benefits that exist today:

1. Universal Value

When you convert one country's money to another country's money, you pay an "exchange rate" because companies that exchange currencies charge a fee for their services. For example, U.S. dollars are worth X number of pesos, pounds, or Australian dollars. This exchange rate fluctuates every day, making it difficult to tell just how much spending power you will have with the exchanged currency.

With cryptocurrencies, there is no exchange rate when you buy or sell a single type of currency, such as Litecoin, for example. As long as you stick with one type of coin, it doesn't matter what country you send it to. Once you and another person online agree to a transaction, you send the money. There is no conversion into any other currency. And there is no fee for sending it.

This means you can buy and sell across international boundaries, without any country taking a piece of it, monitoring the trade, or approving it. This is one of the major ways cryptocurrencies are changing the global economy.

If you exchange one cryptocurrency for another, there will be an exchange rate. But you and your buyer or seller agree on that rate. You can stick with the rate determined by the market, or you can ask for a discount.

2. No One Can Seize Your Assets

When you use a bank or a service like PayPal, the institution can freeze your assets if it thinks your transactions don't meet their standards. You can find yourself scrambling to defend yourself while having no access to your money.

You own your account when trading cryptocurrencies. There is no ruling body to tell you what you can and cannot do with your money. No one can seize your assets.

Now, some people have used this freedom to trade in illegal products, but surely that is not your plan. You can buy and sell legitimate products and services using cryptocurrencies, and no one can tell you how much you can buy or tax the transaction. You may recall that you are anonymous online when your transaction is put into a block chain.

3. No Settlement Period

If you want to get really aggravated, try transferring cash from your bank account to an online brokerage account. The brokerage will hold your funds for three days before it releases them. They call this a "settlement period."

What they will tell you is that the transaction has to be completely verified before you can spend your money. That's right, even for cash. Pretty gutsy of them.

So if you wanted to buy a stock through the brokerage and transferred in cash to do so, you might miss the opportunity because they made you wait three days.

When you send or receive cryptocurrencies, it belongs to the receiver immediately. Take that, brokers.

4. No Identity Theft

It seems like every day you hear about hackers breaking into some company's account and stealing all their customers' credit card and personal information. You are at the mercy of the company's security measures.

You have given them your credit card number, sometimes your Social Security Number or other government identification, and you hope they will take care of it, but often they don't.

You have no such information on file in a cryptocurrency transaction. You own the coins in a private account. Even if hackers broke in and tried to take your coins, the block chain would reject the action because it wouldn't match the other copies of your block that are out there. Read the section on "What Block Chain Means to Cryptocurrency Investors" if you've forgotten how this works.

5. Everyone Has Access

Anyone can get online and trade cryptocurrencies. You don't have to be rich or connected or even experienced. The only time you have to prove anything is when you provide verification of your identity to any exchange you want to sign up with.

Nobody knows exactly what the implications for this peer-to-peer arrangement are. Right now, it looks like people will be buying and selling like they did way back in the day when everyone used cash. You know, like the Middle Ages. Well, maybe not that far back, but it's like buying a lawnmower from your neighbor. You fork over the fifty bucks, and it's yours. Take it home and get to work. The government, the bank, the Federal Trade Commission, and the Securities and Exchange Commission have no way to regulate it.

It's the same with cryptocurrencies. Anyone can go online and buy or sell without anyone else's permission. That's pretty much why the whole system was invented in the first place.

So you see, there are plenty of reasons to expect demand for cryptocurrencies to continue, and to grow. That said, if the supply of coins gets bigger than the demand, you could see prices fall dramatically.

Right now, it's the Wild West out there, so if you start trading cryptocurrencies, stay on top of the trends and read the news. While this paragraph was being written, one cryptocurrency lost 30% of its value.

On the other hand, up until that last paragraph, one cryptocurrency had risen 7500%.

That makes for a nice little transition to our next topic.

The Risks

No book on cryptocurrencies would be complete without a discussion of the risks involved. Like any investment opportunity, you can either make money or lose money. Part of the outcome depends on you and how well you work the market, but at least part of the outcome depends upon prevailing market conditions that help determine a particular cryptocurrency's worth at any given time.

How To Buy Bitcoin

Instability

The first thing you need to think about is that cryptocurrencies are unstable right now. No one can tell if they are a passing fad or the wave of the future. Some people have made huge amounts of profit on them, while other people have lost their entire investment.

This kind of investing is nothing like buying Microsoft stock and holding it for ten years. You can't even be sure if Bitcoin, Litecoin, Ethereum, or any other cryptocurrency will even exist in ten years.

The most important thing to remember is that you shouldn't just buy some crypto coins and then ignore your investment. They will be jumping around in value for some time. If they drop too far, sell and save at least part of your investment. If they soar in value, consider selling and locking in your profits.

Understand that you are getting into a new technology that has yet to prove itself, and plenty of people are skeptical. That doesn't make it bad, but it does make it risky.

Lack of Regulation

One of the strengths of cryptocurrencies is also a major weakness: no one is regulating any of the transactions. While that is attractive to those who want complete freedom in their investing, it also means there is no protection if something goes wrong. Your investment is not insured, and if you get ripped off, there is no one to report it to.

Crooks are swooping down on the cryptocurrency markets, and they can be awfully clever. When I said there are safety measures that prevent theft of a transaction, that's for today. Who knows what sinister hackers will come up with tomorrow?

So don't fall asleep at the wheel. You are the regulator of your transactions, nobody else. Watch for any red flags that make a deal sound too good to be true.

Governments want a piece of the action by collecting capital gains on cryptocurrency trades. That means when you make a profit, you will owe a percentage in taxes. Technically, you already do owe capital gains tax on cryptocurrency profits, but it's not hard to image people hiding their profits to avoid paying taxes. This book is not about cheating on your taxes. It is about possibly making so much money you won't care how much the taxes are.

Tax authorities may still spoil the party. It is hard to imagine how they would tax the millions of trades going on daily in practically every country worldwide, but you just know they are going to try. Bitcoin alone racks up $10 billion in trades every single day, so that's a lot of potential untapped taxable revenue authorities are just itching to get their hands on.

Still, for right now, profits are not regulated very well. It's mostly done on the honor system.

Keep an eye out for regulators to come into the game. This could either help or hurt your trading. The only thing we know for sure is that they are coming.

Price Manipulation

So far, it looks like the marketplace is determining the price of coins. Supply and demand fluctuate, and traders set prices accordingly. However, it is possible someone could start manipulating the price.

A Beginner's Guide to Cryptocurrency Investing

Here's one way they could do it. A person could buy a lot of coins of one currency. Like a LOT. Enough so that one person could have a large percentage of the coins available. Such traders are known in the business as "whales."

Next, the whale might sell all their coins in one big dump. The whale would take their profits, and other traders might panic and sell their coins too, driving the price down even further. Then the original whale could come back into the market and buy up coins at a discount price. This coupled with current demand trends for cryptocurrencies usually drives the price back up especially if everyone piles on and starts buying again. Then the manipulator could sell and take profits again, repeating this cycle over and over.

If someone tried that in the stock market, regulators would bust them and bring criminal charges. But with the unregulated crypto market, you could be at the mercy of these manipulators. There is also early evidence suggesting that automated bot trades are in fact responsible for much of the volatility of the cryptocurrency markets.

My prediction is that something like this will happen very soon, if it is not happening already. In fact, on November 29th of 2017, multiple bots executing large trades of the Chinese cryptocurrency Neo caused a flash crash that plummeted the price per coin from $34 down to $3.74 in a few seconds. The price returned to normal by the end of the trading day, but not before a lot of panicked investors had lost millions of dollars by trading out of the market as it was crashing. Those who sat tight didn't lose a penny. And on December 22, Bitcoin experienced a massive drop in value, almost $5,000 per coin, after a founder of a cryptocurrency website announced he was selling off all his Bitcoins. That triggered a comparable drop in almost all cryptocurrencies, but most have regained their value since then.

One final thing to be aware of is that in the heavily regulated stock markets, there are safety checks in place known as circuit breakers that automatically shut down all trading if market indicators show something is off. There are no such automatic safety checks in the world of cryptocurrencies, so make sure you watch the markets daily and be prepared to act if market conditions indicate a need to make a move.

Spoofing

You won't believe this one. Crooks find a way to get malware into your computer. Then when you type an address to send your purchased coins to, the malware replaces it with another address the bad guys are using.

Check the address just before you press **send** to make sure it is still the right one.

How do these people sleep at night?

Phishing

It's hard to believe this one still works. You get an email from some company, asking you to verify your electronic wallet information. You enter it in their website, including your password, and they steal your coins.

Hacking into Wallet Providers

If you use an online service that provides you a wallet to store your coins, that service can be hacked. It happened in June of 2017, and the hackers got $300,000 before they were stopped.

Your Errors

If you type an address incorrectly, or copy it and leave off the last digit, you could send your coins to nowhere and not be able to get them back. Pay attention. This is a detailed business. Make sure you have your coffee before you trade.

Failure to Store Coins in an Offline Device

If you store your wallet on your computer without backing it up to a hard drive or USB device, a crash could destroy your money. Also, hackers getting into your computer might be able to steal it.

Honestly, this list to watch out for will grow with time. Risks in investing, especially in a new product, are not always clear when you start out.

I have said this before, but only invest money in cryptocurrencies you can afford to lose. Take profits often, and sell losing trades as fast as you can.

Cryptocurrencies may settle down as they become better known, and trading could become more orderly. Until then, you have to be orderly and protect yourself.

The Impact of Cryptocurrencies

Cryptocurrencies have disrupted the way money flows around the globe. In a short span of time, digital coins have toppled government currency policies and eliminated a lot of middlemen that used to keep some people from sending and receiving money.

Let's look at some of the developments:

Remittance Fees

- Remittance Fees

Many countries charge a high fee for sending and receiving money in anything but their own currency. That means people who earn elsewhere and send money home will pay for the privilege.

Cryptocurrencies prevent the country from charging those fees, because the transactions are anonymous. It's impossible to tell who is outside the country and who is inside the country.

Legitimacy

- Legitimacy

Many of Bitcoin's earliest users used the anonymity of the digital currency to engage in illegal activities. But legitimate businesses have increasingly accepted cryptocurrencies and they are gaining in popularity and legitimacy daily. Banks are looking at cryptocurrencies as a new way to transfer funds. Shoppers are using them, and stores are accepting them to pay for online orders.

Cryptocurrency is having a major impact on who does business with who. (That might need to be " whom," but let's don't get stuffy.)

Traditional Currency Values

- Traditional Currency Values

You can find out every day how much the U.S. dollar is worth against the yen, or the pound, and so forth. This is already old-fashioned. Because cryptocurrencies are not tied to the price of gold or any one country's currency, they develop a value based on the marketplace. The ups and downs of digital coins may not even follow specific economies.

Inflation

- Inflation

You've read tales about how much a dollar used to buy, and how much it will buy in the future. For example, $100 today will only buy $75 worth of goods and services in 15 years.

All that assumes that the person earning money spends it on goods in his own country. But what happens when a cryptocurrency buys more than a local denomination of traditional money? Your spending power increases instead of decreases.

In that case, traditional measures of inflation won't mean a thing. Your buying power could go up while people using traditional currencies might buy less. Of course, I said, "could." It's not a guarantee.

A New Way to Create Money

- A New Way to Create Money

You read all the time something like " One percent of the people control fifty percent of the money." Such statements make it sound like there is this one pie of money we are all splitting, and too many rich people are gobbling up more than their fairshare.

But in cryptocurrency there is no pie. There is no set amount of money we must share. Money gets created every day. And this has never been more true than with cryptocurrencies.

If you bought one Bitcoin for $100 when it was young, you could have sold it for $20,000 in 2017. You would have turned your $100 into $20,000. I know I said it twice, but that's to make you stop and think.

If you did what I described, you created more money. The pie just grew, especially if a lot of other people did the same thing. The pie got bigger. You didn't have to grab a piece of someone else's share; you created your own bigger share.

Maybe you've been working too hard. How long would it take you to earn $20,000?

Problems Cryptocurrencies Need to Solve

Cryptocurrencies have grown so fast that it's getting difficult to approve and clear transactions in the block chain. Some businesses that want to use cryptocurrency may be holding off due to the growing time delays in completing transactions.

It sounds like the early days of music file sharing, when Napster came along. At first, a small group of renegades was sharing files, but file-sharing boomed, and today it is commonplace. But the path was rocky as recording artists fought to get paid royalties for file shares, and record companies wanted new laws to protect their copyrighted music and get paid their traditional fees. Congress responded and did protect the interest of the artists and record companies but with concessions that recognized the new file sharing technology. But all this took years.

How To Buy Bitcoin

Maybe we can expect the same for cryptocurrencies. Outlaws used it first, and as legitimate people continue to come into the market, it's clear that the complete lack of regulation may not be protective enough. Keep your ears tuned to the news to learn about new developments in this area. Without some kind of standards for ethics and accuracy, cryptocurrencies will have a hard time growing.

Start-up currencies are multiplying so fast that it's hard to know what to invest in. Bitcoin is the granddaddy, but others like Ethereum are on the rise. Some have already come and gone. The marketplace is a great sifter, separating the wheat from the chaff, and until things settle down, no coin is safe so select your investments carefully.

Right now, it is a "hit and run" market. Get in, make your money, get out and wait for another opportunity. If this type of investment is going to be attractive to a wide audience, it will need to narrow itself down to currencies that have a chance of lasting.

Governments are now charging exchanges exorbitant amounts to start up new cryptocurrencies. This makes it expensive to do and likely will hamper the growth of the industry. Clearing this hurdle means negotiating for fees that are comparable to other business licenses.

The next problem is getting rid of the scammers and people using cryptocurrencies to sell illegal products. Right now, it is almost a wink-wink situation. But that can't continue. Someone is going to have to come up with a way to catch the crooks while allowing everyone else as much freedom as possible.

If this can't be done, cryptocurrencies could go the way of the dinosaurs.

Denominations must be created so you can count your change easily. When Bitcoin hit $20,000, this made it hard to buy things. The seller has to recreate smaller amounts of Bitcoin and send them to you.

Just to make it confusing, spending is called an "input," and the change is called an "output." This is all done in fractions right now. So, for example, you might input a coin worth $1,000 get the output of .85 of a coin back as change.

I don't know about you, but that sounds like a lot of numbers to keep track of. If you get .85 of a coin plus .05 of a coin plus .09 of a coin, is that the right amount? This process is automated in trades right now, but there may be an easier way to do it so that it is more intuitive. The example sounds okay if we start with $1,000, a nice, round number. But how much change should you get back if you spend $1272 and a coin is worth $1567? Should we just trust the automation to give us the right percentages?

Let's hope someone comes up with a way that makes it easier to follow.

Investing Strategies

This section isn't about setting up your account with an exchange, creating a wallet and all that. It's about what to do once you have done those things. It's about having a method for your investing, so you're not just flailing around in the deep end asking for someone to throw you a lifeline.

A Beginner's Guide to Cryptocurrency Investing

The Easy Strategies

So, here are some approaches that are for beginners. You can get all fancy later if you want to, but you don't have to. You could use these approaches as your only way of investing and never change them, if you prefer.

In other words, they work.

Let's get started.

Buy when the coin is stable

This means don't buy when everyone is all excited about how high it has gone. Prices always come back down at some point. Be patient and wait for the price to drop.

Watch for a sideways move on the chart. There is a saying in investing that goes, "Don't try to catch a falling knife." That means when prices are falling, don't just jump in when you think they have fallen enough. Wait until things settle down, and the chart shows the prices moving sideways, many slightly up in a gentle slope.

There, that's better. Your nerves will be calm, and you won't be up at 4 a.m. checking prices.

Use dollar-cost averaging.

This is one of the best ideas since sliced bread. It is so simple, you'll whack your head and say, "duh!"

You pick a dollar amount you will invest every month. Let's just say $100 for our example. Now, you never change the dollar amount. Every month you automatically buy whatever coin it is you are interested in. Don't change coins.

So here's what happens. Let's say the price of the coin goes up next month. Your $100 buys a smaller amount of the coin because it is more expensive.

Then the coin drops the next month. Now your $100 goes a lot further, and you get more of the coin.

Over time, your average cost will be very low. You'll be buying sometimes on the peaks of the chart, sometimes in the valleys, and sometimes in between. It all averages out to a pretty decent price.

This is a strategy you can set up and let it run.

The only thing I would add is to watch the news. If you hear something that makes you think a big crash is coming, then get out.

Invest your spare change.

This one is going to make you mad at me. You're going to scream, "Why didn't you just tell me this instead of reading all that stuff about block chains and miners?"

There are two reasons.

The first is you should never invest in something you don't understand. At this point, you know enough about cryptocurrency investing to watch out for scams, mistakes, trends, and best times to take profits. You're welcome.

How To Buy Bitcoin

The other reason is you really need to be reading more, so I thought I would give you some practice.

All right, here is how you invest your spare change. You join a service, such as Lawnmower or Coinbase. (You have to search for Coinflash, which is attached to Coinbase to get started. You will need accounts with both.) You hook up your checking account to the service. It takes every transaction and rounds it up. So if you spend $3.14, it would round it up to $4.00. Then it would take the $.86-cent difference and invest it into the coin of your choice. A purchase of $5.51 means you put in $.49 for investing.

I know, it's so easy! Makes you want to thump me in the head. That's why my address is not in this book.

But seriously, isn't that simple? You can wade into the waters this way and see how you do.

Most of these services wait until you have $10 before investing. Oh, yeah, and the cost? A buck a month. Sheesh.

If you are using one of the easy strategies, don't keep jumping around from one strategy to another. Why? They each take time to work. Over time, you will see a pattern emerging. If you keep changing strategies, you won't see any kind of pattern, except for pattern baldness from worrying yourself to death. (I hear pattern baldness happens to both males and females, so that joke should work for both sexes.)

The Advanced Strategies

Don't start with these. Use the easy ones, and while you're getting used to investing in cryptocurrencies, study these. Make trades on paper so you can see how you would have done if you had put in real money. Once your confidence is pretty good, try one of these if you want to.

Momentum Trading

This really more like short-term trading than long-term investing. We looked at this when discussing using the MACD indicator in the section called, "Using Trends to Your Advantage." Reread it if you don't remember.

What I want to cover here is how to figure out which coin is good for momentum trading. For this kind of trading, you don't decide on a coin to invest in until you see a certain pattern. Look for a zigzag pattern that is moving sideways or trending slightly upwards.

Your goal is to buy when the price hits the low point and sell when it hits the high point. All of the low points and high points should line up close enough that you can draw a line across them. Draw a line across the peak points on the highs, then draw a line across the lowest points on the lows. That is your trading range.

The trick is to sell every time the price hits the line you drew. Don't get greedy. Expect it to drop like it always has. At some point, it will break up the pattern and you won't be able to draw your nice orderly lines like before. Then it's time to move on to another coin and look for a zigzag pattern in it.

If your coin hits peaks and valleys too fast, you may end up trading so often that the fees are killing you. Pay attention to your costs as you go.

A Beginner's Guide to Cryptocurrency Investing

Diversified Investing

You'll need a pretty good sized investment stash to use this one. The idea is that you buy a little of each coin. Maybe choose a half-dozen that you like, and spread your investment among them.

If one loses money, chances are the others may make up for it.

You have to constantly cull out the losers and find a new place to invest that money.

Buy an ICO

There is a time when you can get into a coin at a low point right at the beginning. This happens during an ICO, which means "initial coin offering." When someone wants to put out a new coin, it happens on a single offering day.

People tend to pile on, driving the price straight up.

Almost every time, that sharp uptick is followed by a deep dip. Some people start taking profits and that drives the price down. That's when you pounce. If the price recovers, as it often does, you can ride out a pretty long profit streak.

A Cutting-Edge Strategy

Now hold on to your hat. You are getting ready to learn about a strategy that can make you a lot more money than simply buying and selling cryptocurrencies.

A new entity has come on the scene. It is a cryptocurrency bank named Change Bank that recently opened in Singapore, and this idea will surely spread.

Here is the idea. The bank stores all types of cryptocurrencies. You can store yours there. Then you can use them to invest in real estate, stocks, bonds, and a myriad of other investments. The bank does this through smart contracts, which are basically direct agreements between you and the seller of the investment. They were made expressly for investing with cryptocurrencies.

Follow me on this. Say you make a tidy little sum on a crypto coin investment. You take your profits. Now, knowing that digital coin investing is high-risk, you decide to put your profits into something less risky so you won't lose them. You buy a property. Basically, you just got a house and lot for free because you bought it with profits from your coin investing.

You keep doing this with all your profits, and you become a regular mogul.

Every time you take your profits, you are left with the original amount you invested in cryptocurrencies. So you keep using that amount to invest in more coins. You could be a money-making machine if you do it right. You'll probably lose on some coin trades, but at least you won't lose the profits, because you took them out.

You don't have to do this with just real estate. Anything anyone invests in is available. The cryptocurrency bank will make the transaction happen, and bam, now you own gold, dividend-paying stocks, interest-paying bonds, and a share in an oil well. None of your friends will be able to stand you.

Shorting

Just a brief word about a practice called "shorting." This is a complicated trade where you actually make money if the price of a coin goes down. You are betting against the market.

You will hear about it as you begin to explore the world of investing in cryptocurrencies.

People do it successfully every day, and some of them make money. In fact, some make money by buying coins as they are going up, and shorting them as they are going down.

It's all very exciting, but it's not for you. This is not a beginner's technique, and you can get burned badly if you don't know what you are doing. People that do know what they are doing often lose money when trying to short the market. So it could be devastating for you.

Start doing regular investing, and when you feel really, really confident, look into shorting. I must tell you though, that even some really seasoned traders don't use this technique. Cryptocurrencies are risky enough without doubling the risk.

Holding Cryptocurrencies in Your IRA

Let's look at your retirement account. If you think the current investments in your IRA are not growing fast enough, you might consider putting some of your investment funds in cryptocurrencies.

If you want to do this, you have to work around the IRS. Don't worry, it's all perfectly legal.

See, a regular IRA isn't allowed to hold cryptocurrencies directly. That's because your IRA must be held by a trustee for your benefit. The trustee is typically a bank or a brokerage. And guess what? They won't allow you to put cryptocurrencies in your retirement account.

Don't worry. We'll eliminate them. What you want to do is open a Checkbook IRA. Shop around for a custodian that allows these. A custodian can be a bank, credit union, or a trust company. So what happens is your Checkbook IRA owns a limited liability company (LLC), and you appoint yourself the manager of that LLC.

You can invest in anything you want.

There is some paperwork involved, and rules to follow. One of those rules is you must make all purchases in the name of the LLC. That means you would need to set up an account with an exchange in the name of the LLC. Not all of them allow this, but enough do, so shop around. It is prohibited for you to transfer cryptocurrencies held in your name to your IRA.

Most sellers want your real name, and I just told you to only buy in the name of the LLC if you want to put the coins in your IRA. You can get around this opening your exchange account like this: John Smith, As Manager of ABC LLC. Obviously, you put your LLC name instead of the "ABC" in the example.

Most exchanges will store your coins in a wallet for you. But if you want to transfer those coins to your own wallet, be sure the wallet is in the name of your LLC.

To save yourself some headaches, here is what you MUST do. Get a full-service custodian to not only open your Checkbook IRA, but also draw up the paperwork and guide you through how to make your transactions. Rules are going to be changing rapidly, and you need someone who keeps up with all that stuff.

Oh, by the way, if you have a 401(k), you don't have to worry about all rules for IRAs. If you want to, though, you can set up an LLC that is tied to your 401(k).

A Beginner's Guide to Cryptocurrency Investing

A Word About Charts

You really need to know a little bit about how to read price charts. There are a lot of free chart services out there. Trading View is just one of them, but it will serve our purposes for this discussion.

You can choose the coin you want to see a chart on, and there it is, big as life right on your screen. The best part, though, is if you scroll down, on the left you will see a pro trader's take on the chart. It is very helpful. No trader is always right, but you can learn from the tips you find here.

You should really study charts for the stock market, too. The same principles apply when charting stocks as when charting coins. The Crypto Stache offers a beginner's guide to reading charts, and it is free. You can become a VIP member and get charts and tips specific to cryptocurrencies.

Charts are not as complicated as they seem at first glance, and having a visual representation of what a coin or stock is doing really straightens out your thinking. They also help keep your emotions in check.

Tax Considerations

Each country sets up its own tax rules, but I will use the United States Internal Revenue Service to give you a rundown on cryptocurrency taxes.

The IRS doesn't treat cryptocurrencies as money. It treats them as property, just like real estate. Why? Because their primary goal is to confuse taxpayers.

Here's what this means for you. If you buy coins and sell them in less than a year, you will pay tax on the profits at the same rate as your regular income tax.

If you sell the coins after one year or more, you will pay capital gains tax. This will be a different rate than your regular income tax. It could be more or it could be less, depending on what Congress decides.

All trades from one kind of digital coin to another kind digital coin are taxed, unless you hold the original coin for more than a year.

Now, coin traders have been known for not reporting their transactions on their tax returns. However, the IRS sued one exchange, Coinbase, and won the right to view all of their transaction records. The Wild West is about to get tamed.

If your coins are in an IRA, the taxes are deferred until you are in retirement and start drawing out money. Except a Roth IRA is reversed. You get taxed on your money, then put it into a Roth IRA, and you don't owe taxes when you pull it out.

Here are how some other jurisdictions tax cryptocurrencies:

European Union: No tax on cryptocurrencies, but each country in the union can make its own tax rules.

The U.K.: Taxes cryptocurrencies at the same rate as foreign currencies, but "speculative" transactions are not vulnerable to any tax.

Germany: If you sell the coins in less than a year, you pay a 25% tax. If you hold the coins longer than a year and then sell them, there is no tax due.

Japan: Taxes cryptocurrency trading as business income.

Australia: Businesses that accept cryptocurrencies pay a value-added tax. Private individuals can make purchases with digital coins tax-free if the value is less than AUD 10.00. Trades of these currencies are taxed like stock trading.

If you're not in one of these countries, check your government's approach to taxing cryptocurrencies.

The Future

At this point, trying to determine what the future will bring for cryptocurrencies might require the use of a crystal ball. But we have enough information to offer some educated speculation about where digital money is heading.

Purchases

You can already buy goods in an online "crypto only" store. This trend could revolutionize retail operations. Authors are selling books in crypto stores, and entrepreneurs are selling all kinds of goods and services.

You may not remember, but in the early days of the Internet, people didn't trust it enough to buy things online. Now such purchases are commonplace.

Crypto buying could go the same way. Buying with traditional currencies might just be one of a hundred options you have. Maybe stores will run specials offering discounts if you use a certain coin to pay for your purchases.

Values of Coins

The values of cryptocurrencies are vague right now, but they may be easier to value in the future. Compare digital coins to stocks. When you buy a stock, you own part of the company. You can do research on that company to learn about its earnings, sales, growth and new products. The stock gets valued by investors based on these fundamentals.

Cryptocurrencies have no fundamentals right now. They are popular because, well, because they are popular. The demand for them is driving the prices. But in the near future, each currency may find its own specialty. For example, Bitcoin could become the cryptocurrency to use for faster processing, Ethereum could be best for smart contracts (digitally executed agreements with no humans involved), and XRP already acts as a bridge between different currencies for easy trading and conversion.

If these sorts of developments happen, each coin will have a value based on how many trades it handles, or how big the business deals are that use it as a currency, and so on. Some solid numbers that show values of the trades conducted could give cryptocurrencies a foundation to base prices upon. This is something experienced Wall Street people will want to see.

Winners, Losers, and Newcomers

A Beginner's Guide to Cryptocurrency Investing

Experts predict that Bitcoin and Ethereum will survive, but many currencies won't. That doesn't mean there will be only two, but some are going to dominate. Other cryptocurrencies may disappear, taking their investors' money with them.

Banks may issue their own cryptocurrencies, requiring any bank or individual to convert to that currency for transactions. (Let's make a wild guess. The banks will charge for that conversion.)

Privacy

Exchanges will be pressured to reveal identities of traders for tax reasons, while traders will try to remain anonymous and continue to shield the details of actual transactions in the block chain. It wouldn't be surprising to see exchanges open in countries where coin trades are not taxed, and then keep their customers' identities secret. The IRS would have a hard time forcing a foreign business to give up their records.

The coming years will be about regulators wanting transparency, and the block chain trying to remain anonymous. I mean, there are bad people trying to hide their transactions, so transparency is not an entirely unreasonable goal. However, for every terrorist you catch, someone else who is innocent gets their information exposed, and perhaps they are arrested on what turn out to be unwarranted charges, just because a trade looked unusual.

Or what if, without your knowledge, you end up in a transaction with a human trafficker's account? Will you be subject to investigation? Will you be able to prove you had no knowledge of the other person's activities?

Getting Recognized

The next boom may come when governments officially recognize a digital coin as its preferred currency. If a domino effect happens, where one government after another legitimizes Bitcoin, Ethereum, or some other coin, that would be a game-changer.

Higher education is already recognizing cryptocurrencies by offering classes on them, and some are accepting cryptocurrencies as a way to pay tuition and conduct other transactions with the schools.

Some companies are investing in cryptocurrencies as a way to make more money, further adding to the air of legitimacy for these coins. But these currencies will need to attract some serious institutional players to survive. When big companies start relying on cryptocurrencies for conducting business, we may be off to the races. Digital coins may take over and become our standard way of buying and selling.

Does all this guarantee that cryptocurrency is the future of money? Well, no. However, if you understand the pattern for society accepting a new technology, some signs are there.

Technology Adoption Patterns

When a new technology comes along, it is first used by "early adopters," tech-savvy people who are always on the lookout for the next big thing in tech. Next comes the second wave of people who don't like to get in early, but like to keep up with technology. Then next, the technology goes mainstream and stays that way until something replaces it.

You can see this pattern in cryptocurrency now. The early adopters have been using it for some time, more people have crept into the market, and now it is on the verge of going mainstream. That is, if the pattern holds up.

So what will happen to paper money? Think about music for a moment. CDs took over the market at one point, replacing vinyl. Then online file sharing made it possible to download a digital copy with no need for a CD, and streaming now allows people to listen to "internet radio stations."

But, CDs are still around. You can still buy them, and people still have CD players. Paper money may end up being like that. It might be something you only use on occasion. You might keep some so you can pop into the local drugstore, but your serious money might be in cryptocurrencies.

Paychecks

If at some point in the future you get paid on your job with cryptocurrencies, how will you know how much money you have? Your new coins could lose value overnight. Or they might soar. Will cryptocurrency ever be stable enough to become the most popular choice for paying wages?

Of course, it could be the dollar that plummets in value. There may come a time when no worker will want to get paid in dollars.

This is a tough one. Sometimes it is hard to imagine all the potential applications and implications of a new technology.

Artificial Intelligence

Imagine you have your own online bot that learns about your tastes, fears, and desires and starts trading for you. Because artificial intelligence can analyze tons more data than you can, it could understand the cryptocurrency market's current condition and trends and make investment choices you might never imagine.

One of the things that makes markets work is that someone is always wrong. Someone sells thinking a price is headed down, and the buyer sees the price go up on the new purchase. If everyone has their own smart bot, will there be bad trades in the cryptocurrency market? Every trend would be recognized by everybody at the same moment. Who would you buy from if everyone thought the market was going up? No one would be selling.

Perhaps the cryptocurrency market would become a boring place without many ups and downs-and few investment opportunities because of that. With no market inefficiencies, opportunists wouldn't have any place to jump in.

Your Life in a Block Chain

In this book, we have learned that a block chain stores all transactions for buying and selling cryptocurrencies. Every computer node on the block chain system gets an exact copy of every transaction, making block chains one of the most secure technologies ever invented.

Now, what if a block chain gets used for birth and death records, marriage licenses, to record what properties changed hands, the repair history on your car, and how much sugar is being sold in the world?

Assuming the identity of everybody is kept secret in the chain, we would have a lot of information about ourselves and others that could instantly tell us how our society is doing, even how the whole human race is doing.

The idea of taking a census would seem old-fashioned, because we would already know how many people there were and where they lived. We would be able to send money instantly when a disaster strikes anywhere. We could find the best price on any commodity worldwide. We could divert resources to the poor faster than we ever dreamed.

Let your mind wander a bit, and you can see that block chain technology has the potential to be about much more than simply trading Bitcoins.

Block Chain May Change the Way We Work

If the block chain "knows" everything, there won't be much demand for workers with a lot of knowledge. College graduates won't need memory; they will need creativity. What will be in demand are so-called right brain activities. Creative thinking will be the best way to get ahead in a firm.

Here are some possibilities:

Imaginative Strategies

People who can predict future demand for products and services will get great jobs. Employees will need to think long-term and come up with strategies to take advantage of what will be happening five and ten years out. This is because technology will be changing the business environment so quickly that today's strategies will need to be replaced regularly.

Already, sites such as Springwise and Long Bets are testing people's abilities to make predictions. You can test your predictions against reality, noting which ones worked and which ones didn't.

Humans won't be needed to gather data; they will be needed to steer the company toward a future that is still being imagined.

Rethinking the Present

Even current practices in a business will need to be challenged. "We've always done it that way" will no longer be a valid reason to keep the status quo; it will be the main reason to change it.

In the future, there may be a job such as a professional questioner, a person who is trained to ask the right questions to find ways to revamp policies and procedures. This may become less of an art and more of a science. Universities might even offer questioning courses.

This will all happen because we won't need to focus on outdated data. The block chain will update the world every time a new piece of data is generated. And because the competition will all have the same data, innovation will become a mad race to find new ideas.

Creative Problem Solving

In response to all those pertinent questions a professional questioner comes up with, someone will need to create solutions unearthed by the inquiry. A creative problem solver may use information from unrelated industries or surprising sources to develop innovative solutions.

Maybe their proposed solutions will need to be approved by a committee, or, in the spirit of the decentralized block chain, maybe the problem solver will be free to try out the solution without seeking permission from anyone first.

Adapting Quickly

Unexpected events are bound to happen in this atmosphere of rapid change. People who can think on their feet and come up with instant strategies may be in demand. This could be a leader who is prepared to restructure an entire organization in response to an unforeseen development.

The old, traditional governing board is going to have to have some emergency meetings to keep up with changes in future business environments. And nimble startups may takeover where slow companies fail to adapt.

Bouncing Back

There could be a lot of failures in this environment. As new ideas are tried out, they may be wrong or need adjusting. People who can bounce back from failure will be valuable on the job. In fact, failure may become a good thing because it will show the person is trying out new ideas.

Yogi Berra once said, "The future ain't what it used to be." Perhaps this means the future is going to be much different than we might have imagined just a few short years ago.

Possibilities are opening up that once seemed like impossibilities.

This is a book about investing in cryptocurrencies, but you can see how block chain technology that makes digital coin trades possible is making a lot of other things possible as well. If you decide to invest, you are investing in the future.

You can't help but wonder what a Thomas Edison or Benjamin Franklin would say if they could see how things are today. Even someone as recent as Steve Jobs would be surprised. Heck, I'm surprised, and I'm still alive.

Conclusion

At this point, you know quite a lot about investing in cryptocurrencies. Maybe you feel like you know too much. If words and concepts are swimming around in your head, don't worry. Once you get started, it will all make sense.

Reread sections of this book to refresh your memory. Study the market charts, and start making trades on paper. You will see how you would have done with real money.

But there is something one final thing you must understand that is just as important as understanding the market. You need to understand yourself. Each person has a unique risk tolerance. Some will lie awake fretting over a $100 investment, while another sleeps like a baby after investing $50,000.

Don't try to change your risk tolerance because you think you should be braver or somehow more mature. Your instincts could be right on. In fact, for you, they are.

You might change how you feel about things as you gain more knowledge and experience, but don't force it. If your gut is screaming, "Wait a minute!" then wait.

A Beginner's Guide to Cryptocurrency Investing

Also learn to listen to that voice inside you that says, "This is a good trade." That's right, there is a positive instinct as well as a negative one. If you find yourself getting really excited about a trade and rushing to get into it that is emotion taking over, not instinct. Instinct is calm and wise. It comes from considering all the possibilities, then making a decision.

Stay off the emotional roller coaster. Don't make investing decisions based on fear or greed.

You are going to make mistakes. Either that, or you are the greatest trader in history. Warren Buffett has made mistakes. So expect it. Sometimes you will have to take some losses. Don't hesitate to sell if you think a coin's price is going even lower than it is now, even if you have already lost money. Take the blow and live to fight another day. Hanging on in desperate hope while your money disappears is the absolute worst way to live.

But don't panic, either. Make a level-headed decision. Strong emotions are your enemy.

Knowing yourself also means choosing the best investment style for you. If you are the kind of person who likes to tinker with your investments often, then some of the advanced strategies may be for you. If you prefer not to feel like you need to watch investments constantly, choose one of the easier strategies.

There is not one right strategy and a wrong one. So choose the one that fits your personality. At first, you may try a couple of strategies. But after that initial period, pick one strategy and stick with it. That is the best way to learn it.

And another thing. Stay out of the crowd. If your friends and colleagues start expressing opinions about the cryptocurrency market, keep your head. You don't want to be one of the lemmings running off the cliff. (Lemmings really do that, you know. They commit mass suicide.)

Be your own person, and make decisions you understand. Never, ever buy a coin you don't understand, make a trade that confuses you, or flip a coin to decide whether to buy or sell. Trade only when you know what you are doing and why.

Now for my best piece of advice. Become a student of the cryptocurrency market. The environment is changing so rapidly that yesterday's learning is outdated in no time. Stay up to date on the news in this area. Join a cryptocurrency investing club. Watch television broadcasts about the latest news.

Read online, but don't try to follow everyone's advice. You will find that many of them disagree with each other. Don't choose a strategy just because some famous blogger says that is the way to go. Trust yourself, and trust your learning.

You'll be keeping up with one of the most exciting things to hit the world in a long time. You will be participating in the future, watching it come alive.

While we are talking about learning, make sure you know about other types of investments as well. Cryptocurrencies should not be anyone's only investment. It is too high-risk for that. You need some money in some lower-risk investments like bonds, and some in medium-risk investments like stocks. You might put other funds in real estate or even gold. Also look at mutual funds and exchange-traded funds.

Keep your learning broad, and work on understanding the investment world as a whole.

Back to cryptocurrencies. Look at quite a few different ones and try to understand what they are for. Each has its own niche in the marketplace. But at some point, pick only one to start with. Stick with that one until you get used to anticipating ups and downs. Also pay attention to how the news affects your particular cryptocurrency. When Bitcoin dropped 30%, Ethereum hit an all-time high. These coins don't move together in a pack. Economic and political developments could affect each coin differently.

Finally, prepare yourself. Use this book as a reference while you dive into the cryptocurrency world. You will be armed with knowledge and a rational approach to investing.

So off you go, out into the world of investing in cryptocurrencies. Be smart, be wise, and reread this book often.

Isn't it a great time to be alive

DISCLAIMER

The information in this book is intended to improve beginning investors' understanding of putting money into cryptocurrencies. Nothing in this book constitutes investment, legal, or tax advice. The information in this book should not be construed as any endorsement, recommendation or sponsorship of any company, strategy, investment, cryptocurrency coin, or exchange. There are risks in relying on information found on this book, and you must be sure you understand these risks before using any information in this book. You should evaluate the information made available in this book, and you should seek the advice of professionals to evaluate any information, opinions, services, products or other information found herein.

REFERENCE PAGE

This section is created to make sure you make it to the correct sites with ease, affiliate codes may be attached.

Cryptocurrency Mastermind Facebook Group: https://www.facebook.com/groups/mastermindscryptogroup/

Coinbase: Convert Fiat Money into Cryptocurrency
https://www.coinbase.com/join/5942f4464b12f702632679a4

Coinigy: All-In-One Platform For Digital Currency – Trade On 45+ Exchanges From One Secure Account, Also Great For Technical Analysis.
https://www.coinigy.com/?r=28c5aa55

Binance: Favorite Exchange to Trade Altcoins
https://www.binance.com/?ref=10270010

www.ingramcontent.com/pod-product-compliance
Lightning Source LLC
Chambersburg PA
CBHW062206220526
45470CB00009B/2947